Jesus and His Message

AN INTRODUCTION TO THE GOOD NEWS

REV. LEO T. MAHON

Jesus and His Message
An Introduction to the Good News
Rev. Leo T. Mahon

Leo T. Mahon is a priest of the Archdiocese of Chicago. He is well known as an innovative pastor, preacher and retreat master. Fr. Mahon spent many years as a missionary in Panama, where he helped form some of the first basic Christian communities.

Edited by Gregory F. Augustine Pierce
Cover design by Tom A. Wright
Page design and typesetting by Garrison Publications

The artwork on the front cover, "Jesus Healing," is a 150-year-old Greek icon, artist unknown, from the collection of Tim and Jean Unsworth (photo by Jean Morman Unsworth).

Copyright © 2000 by Leo T. Mahon
Published by: ACTA Publications
              Assisting Christians To Act
              4848 N. Clark Street
              Chicago, IL 60640-4711
              773-271-1030

Library of Congress Catalog Number: 99-97623
ISBN: 0-87946-211-6
Year: 04 03 02 01 00
Printing 8 7 6 5 4 3 2
Printed in the United States of America

CONTENTS

DEDICATION

To all those, from my parents on,

who encouraged me to

"strive first for the kingdom of God."

Introduction

We are all familiar with images of Jesus as a baby lying in a manger and as a near-naked man dying on a cross, yet do we really know who he was and what he stood for? Part of the problem is that the events of Jesus' life on earth occurred two thousand years ago. Just as we cannot see objects in outer space without a telescope, we need a lens to look at Jesus and his words. The lens we need is an awareness of the times and culture in which Jesus lived. In this book, I tell the story of Jesus, a "first-century, second-temple" Jew, who lived in the country we now call Israel under the rule of the ancient Romans.

Jesus was a human being. Make no mistake about that. In fact, early church councils condemned as heresy the idea that he was not fully human, just as they taught that he was also fully divine. Each human being is a mystery we cannot hope to understand without knowing his or her historical context. Otherwise, we run the risk of reconstructing the person in our own image or in a manner that suits our own needs. If we do that to Jesus, it is tantamount to idolatry—creating our own image of God.

The chapters in this book are a distillation of my fifty years as a priest trying to explain the essence of the good news to people from Chicago to Panama, in English and in Spanish, in poor and middle-class parishes. I have tried to use the best of scholarly works on Jesus to deepen my own understanding, but I realize that some of my interpretations are open to criticism. All well and good. I do not for one moment expect or want this to be the last word you read on Jesus. Rather, I hope that this little book will inspire you to read the Bible and many other books in an effort to decide, along with John the Baptizer and so many other millions of people over the centuries, whether Jesus is "the one who is to come" (Matthew 11:3).

Of one thing, however, I am certain. The key to understanding Jesus and his message lies in the phrase "the kingdom of God" or "the reign of God." That is the term and image he used to describe and proclaim his vision. If we ignore or misunderstand what Jesus meant by "the kingdom" (and I submit that we have often done so), then we can inadvertently pervert his dream and his mission.

If you read this book alone, please do so slowly and prayerfully. It would be even better, in my mind, if you are able to read and discuss it with others. As a missionary in Panama and a pastor in Chicago, I have seen the power of small groups of people sharing the Jesus story among themselves and recommitting themselves to the Christian movement to bring about the kingdom "on earth as it is in heaven" (Matthew 6:10). To this end, I have included some "Questions for Reflection or Discussion" at the end of each chapter. There are no right or wrong answers to these questions. They are designed to get you thinking about who Jesus is in your own life and how you can better help carry out his vision of the way the world should be.

May God guide you on your journey as you meet (or meet again, as if for the first time) the most exciting person who ever lived and listen (or listen once again, as if for the first time) to his message.

CHAPTER ONE

Jesus and His Message

Who is Jesus to you? What was his message? In what ways does your faith make a difference in how you live your daily life? For some people, Jesus was a great religious teacher and nothing more. For others, he is "the way, the truth, and the life" (John 14:6), the Messiah, the Son of God. This chapter studies the portrait of Jesus painted by the evangelists in the four gospels and invites you to examine your own personal image of Jesus.

Suppose you are coming out of a supermarket on Saturday morning when a friend comes up to you and says, "Everybody is talking about you." What would you do? Would you say, "That's nice," and walk away? I don't think so. You would ask your friend, "What are they saying?"

The same was true of the man we call Jesus of Nazareth. He had a message to deliver, a vision to impart, a dream to share, and he was eager to find out if he was getting through to people. He asked his disciples who people thought he was, what they thought he stood for.

"Some say John the Baptist, but others Elijah, and still others Jeremiah or one of the prophets" (Matthew 16:14), they answered. Now, we know that John had recently been beheaded by King Herod, and Elijah and Jeremiah had been dead for centuries. In a way, people were probably saying that Jesus was *like* those great men of Jewish history, but these answers were of no interest to Jesus. He looked his followers squarely in the eyes and asked, "But who do you say that I am?" (Matthew 15:16). Here for the disciples—as it ultimately is for every Christian—is the bottom-line question. What do we really think about Jesus? Who do we really think he is? What do we think his message was all about? What does our answer mean for how we live our lives?

Simon Peter, always the most impetuous of all the disciples, blurted out, "You are the Messiah, the Son of the living God" (Matthew 16:16). You'd think Jesus would have been glad to hear Peter's answer. We Christians believe that Jesus was, in fact, the Messiah, and at some level Jesus must have known this himself. But we can also imagine that a dark cloud might have come over Jesus' face when he heard it.

Jesus tells Peter and the others to clam up: "And he sternly ordered them not to tell anyone about him" (Mark 8: 30). You see, "messiah" was a truly dangerous word in those days. The popular image of "the Messiah" was that of an insurrectionist, an armed revolutionary who would lead the people in revolt against the hated Romans and win freedom for the Jews. The Romans would execute anyone who claimed to be "the Messiah." In fact, historical records show that in Jesus' own lifetime there were at least two "messiahs" who were crucified.

More than fear for his life was operating here, however. Jesus himself hated the popular Jewish concept of the Messiah and all it stood for: power, violence, war, bloodshed. In fact, he went out of his way to say the opposite. "From that time on, Jesus began to show his disciples that he must go to Jerusalem and undergo great suffering at the hands of the elders and chief priests and scribes, and be killed, and on the third day be raised" (Matthew 16:21).

Peter was aghast, just as we might have been. Who wants to follow a dead messiah? A dead messiah was, by Peter's definition, a failure. Peter says, "God forbid it, Lord! This must never happen to you!" (Matthew 16:22). Jesus responded with one of his strongest statements in the Scriptures. "Get behind me, Satan! You are a stumbling block to me: for you are setting your mind not on divine things but on human things" (Matthew 16:23).

We can almost see Peter's ears turn red. Jesus was telling the disciples that they were wrong in thinking that his message was the key to worldly success. That's thinking the way the devil thinks, not the way God thinks, Jesus told them.

GETTING IT WRONG

But Peter wasn't the only one who got it wrong. Every attempt to label or define Jesus during his lifetime was off the mark. It began when he returned to his hometown of Nazareth at the beginning of his public ministry. He had already become famous as a teacher and healer, but this was his first return since then. At first, his fellow Nazarenes were impressed: "All spoke well of him and were amazed at the gracious words that came from his mouth" (Luke 4:22).

But then they immediately tried to pigeonhole him. Wasn't this Joseph and Mary's son? Hadn't they known him since he was a little boy? Wasn't he really one of them? Shouldn't he be doing his healing here in town? Maybe they could all profit from his fame in some way. Jesus would have none of that. He was not just a local-boy-made-good. His mission was to the entire world, not just to Nazareth or Galilee or even all of Israel. "Truly I tell you, no prophet is accepted in the prophet's hometown" (Luke 4:24), he proclaimed.

That did it. His friends and neighbors immediately turned on him and threw him out of town. If

Jesus wouldn't be who they wanted him to be, then they would have none of him. In fact, Luke relates that they were so mad at him that they took him to "hurl him off the cliff" (Luke 4: 29), but Jesus got away.

But if his friends and neighbors (and later even some of his own family) didn't know what to make of him, even less did his enemies. They called him an impostor, a fake, a charlatan, a destroyer of faith and tradition. They accused him of casting out demons by the power of Beelzebub, which was a horrendous charge at the time. They were all wrong, of course, but so have many been wrong about him down through the ages, even to our own day.

Jesus is arguably the most famous person in all of human history. Certainly his name is the most called upon—both reverently and irreverently. Not even counting the Bible, more books have been written about him than any other personality. Every year we see more of them, ranging from great works of scholarship to popular devotional books. He initiated a movement in a small corner of the ancient world with no more than a hundred followers that has grown into a phenomenal force of more than one billion people who call themselves "Christians."

So it is important for those of us who claim to follow Jesus to ask the question: Who is he, really?

GETTING IT RIGHT

Suppose that a young woman graduate student from, say, China decides to write a book about Franklin Delano Roosevelt. At first, this woman will know little about Roosevelt except that he was an important figure in American and world history. But in order to really understand him, she will have to make an exhaustive study of the first half of the twentieth century. She will have to understand what "Democrat" and "Great Depression" and "New Deal" mean. She must learn about Hitler and Churchill and Stalin and the second world war. She will also have to know about Roosevelt's family life, his mother's influence, his bout with polio. Roosevelt's is a fascinating story, but only a person who has done his or her homework can tell it well.

The same is true of Jesus' story, although the amount of historical documentation of his life is minuscule compared to what is available on Roosevelt. Still, no reputable scholar would deny the following facts. Jesus was a Jew who came from Nazareth, a small town in the Galilee section of the country of Israel, which was then called Palestine. As a young rabbi, he gained a reputation as a healer, wonder-worker and teacher, but his views got him into trouble with both the Jewish and the Roman authorities. He was tried, condemned, crucified and died in Jerusalem, and his followers claimed he had risen from the dead.

A small group of his disciples—including his own mother—formed around his person and vision, and his message spread quickly over the ancient Roman world. It was one of the most rapid and stunning movements in history. It is this movement we must understand if we are to understand Jesus.

THE KINGDOM IS THE MESSAGE

Christianity is not so much a set of doctrines and moral teachings as it is a movement in history—one that is still in motion. What kind of movement? Where is it going...and why? If we want to be honest, responsible, mature followers of Jesus, we must know what his message was and what his movement is trying to accomplish.

The heart of the message of Jesus was the classic Hebrew dream of the "kingdom" or "reign" of God. "Strive first for the kingdom of God and his righteousness, and all these things will be given to you as well" (Matthew 6:33), he said. So there's our starting point and theme for this book. We will strive to understand together what Jesus meant by "the kingdom of God" or "the kingdom of heaven."

From the beginning, however, I wish to state that the kingdom of God is perhaps the most misunderstood teaching of Jesus. First of all, he clearly did not mean that God would somehow be a king like Louis XIV or even one of the modern monarchs. The kingdom of God is much more a state of affairs—a way of relating to others, if you will—than a political entity. Even the word "kingdom" is a problem today, because it implies that God is male, which is not the case. God is pure spirit, of course, which can be neither male nor female.

Also, Jesus was not speaking of the afterlife or the place where good people go after death. Certainly, Jesus believed in eternal life. He spoke about it many times. But this is not what Jesus was talking about when he said, "In fact, the kingdom of God is among you" (Luke 17:21).

Allow me to point out a human situation that will help us understand Jesus' idea of the kingdom or reign of God. Let's say you are a loving parent of seven children. You are dying of cancer and have but a few days to live. You gather your adult children around your bed to bid them farewell. Perhaps one is disabled, another is very troubled and has been in and out of jail, and a third is a single parent struggling to raise three children. The others have good marriages and healthy children and are in good financial shape.

What dying wish would you express, then, to your seven children. I believe you might say something like this: "Love one another. Be good to one another, especially to those of you who need more care. Always forgive one another. Never give up on one another. Stay together as a family. If you do all this, you will be living the way I want you to live."

Now, suppose your children responded positively and permanently to your dying request. Over the years, they would become a beautiful family, saving themselves from discord and ruin and inspiring other families to do the same. But if your children ignored your words and refused your dying request, the results would be tragic. Those children who needed loving care from the others would not get it and would sink into despair and bitterness. Those who were well off would become more and more selfish and self-righteous. All of your grandchildren would grow up in a poisonous atmosphere. The evil would grow fast and last for a long time.

Thus it is with the kingdom of God. If human parents want good things for their loved ones, would that not also be the desire of God, who Jesus taught us was most like a loving parent? It is the will of God that all human beings live now—in this world—in peace as members of the same family, forgiving one another, sharing with one another, taking care of the ones who need it most, regarding all members of the family as valuable and as equals. That is what Jesus meant by the kingdom of God, and that is why he said it had already begun in his person.

Jesus proclaimed this kingdom, lived it, and died for it. And he asked his followers to proclaim it, to live it, and—if necessary—even to die for it. Jesus promised that if they did, someday the entire world would be the way God would have things. What a magnificent world that would be. It would be like...well, it would be like heaven!

And it has already begun.

Questions for Reflection or Discussion

1. How has your image of Jesus changed over your lifetime? What events or experiences have caused the changes?

2. If you were one of the original disciples, how do you think you would have reacted to Jesus' prediction of his suffering, death and rising from the dead? How do you react to it now?

3. How would you describe the kingdom of God? In what ways does your belief in the kingdom influence how you live your daily life?

CHAPTER TWO

Jesus and the Father

How do you imagine God? The great majority of people in the world believe in God, but their images or ideas of God vary drastically. Jesus had a very specific concept of God, one that was based on the tradition of the Hebrew people but was much more personal, to the point that he called God "Abba, Father" (Mark 14:36). This chapter explains Jesus' teachings about God and presents some challenging ideas to help you clarify and possibly broaden your understanding of God.

What are the over-riding values in your life? By what principle or principles do you live? For whom or what would you risk—or even sacrifice—your life? When you can answer these questions, you will know the God or god or gods you truly believe in!

For some, Paul said, "Their god is the belly" (Philippians 3:19). We all know people who live to eat. Others worship money—they can and do kill for it. Some people want sex or excitement or prestige or power or even religion more than anything else. They have found their gods.

We Christians say we worship the one, true God. But where did we learn about this God? It is the faith of our spiritual forebears, a precious legacy handed down from them. Most of us received our faith from our immediate ancestors—our parents, grandparents, great grandparents and so on. But preceding them were the Jewish people, the ancient Hebrews, from whom we all learned of the existence and nature of our God.

Who is the God of the Jews and of the Christians and of the Muslims as well? He is the God of Jesus of Nazareth, whom we follow as Christ—"the Anointed One." The Hebrews had anticipated the birth of "the Messiah" for many centuries, and Christians believe that Jesus was the one they were looking for, even though many Jews of his time did not accept him then and do not do so today. (Remember, however, that the first disciples of Jesus were all Jews, that Jesus himself was a Jew, and that the Jews remain God's "chosen people.")

The God of the ancient Hebrews is the same God we Christians believe in, and Jesus learned about this God from his Jewish mother and father, from his extended Jewish family, from the rabbis who surely taught him as he was growing up. "And Jesus increased in wisdom and in years, and in divine and human favor" (Luke 2:52), the gospels tell us.

THE IDOLS OF THE ANCIENT WORLD

No people in history have had an experience with God richer or deeper than that of the Hebrew people. But before we get to the question of who God was for them, let us ask who God was *not* for them.

The ancient Hebrews were surrounded by people who were often more powerful and culturally advanced than they were—such as the Egyptians, the Babylonians, and later the Greeks and Romans, who had very different notions of the divine. Some of Israel's neighbors worshipped the sun, the moon, the seasons, sacred trees. The Hebrews, however, rejected such notions. In their minds, it was God who made everything. How could things then be gods?

Many of the Hebrews' neighbors made images and worshipped them. The main false gods, or idols, were three in number: sex, money and power. Wherever the Hebrews traveled, they encountered along the road or high on the hills above them figures carved from stone or wood and made to look like a penis—the male generative organ. It was an ancient way of saying that the sacred can be found wherever there is fertility and pleasure. The Hebrews believed that fertility is important—both for humans and for our animals and crops. But their

God was far greater than the physical act of procreation alone.

A second idol in the ancient world was wealth or money. The Hebrews' neighbors said that material abundance—especially in the form of gold—was a sure sign of divine favor. So they made statues of gold and silver and fell down to worship them. They also wore gold and silver amulets around their necks and arms and wrists to show that they were in favor with the gods. Our Hebrew ancestors replied that it's good to have money but that wealth is no sign of the presence of God and certainly is not God.

The third and most dangerous idol was power. All over the ancient world, kings, pharaohs, emperors, generals built huge monuments to themselves, claiming divine backing for their power. In Roman times, a large statue of Caesar was erected in almost every city and town. People were encouraged and expected to worship the emperor. For the Jews, these statues were an abomination, and they obstinately refused to bow down to them. Their God was the only one who had the power to control everyone and everything in all creation.

These three—sex, money and power—were the idols that bedeviled the ancient world. Do they still tempt us? Of course, they do. You can see the sex idol in newspapers and magazines—using sex and even soft-core pornography to sell a wide variety of products from cars to clothing. The worship of money is as strong as ever. In medieval Europe, for example, it was forbidden to build a structure higher and bigger than the local church, the "house of God." In our cities today, the tallest buildings are those of banks, insurance companies and other big businesses. The worship of power goes on with horrific consequences for the human race. Millions of lives have been sacrificed on altars erected in honor of Stalin, Hitler and numerous others who would make themselves into gods.

Not only do these ancient idols still permeate modern society, but they are also part of our daily lives. We are constantly tempted to dominate others—spouses, children, neighbors, employees. We have an itch for money—more and more of it. And unless we discipline ourselves we can become slaves to all the pleasures of the flesh.

HEAVEN AND EARTH

Some contemporaries of the ancient Hebrews practiced a dualistic religion. That is, they believed that there was a good god and an evil god—or, more often, good gods and evil gods. For them, human beings were caught in an eternal struggle between the forces of evil and the forces of good. The Hebrews, on the other hand, maintained that there is but one God and that God is good. If there is evil in the world (and there surely is, the Jews believed), then that evil comes from us and not from God.

This pagan view of the spirit world still persists, even among Christians. Haven't you heard the following? "I don't know what got into me. It must have been the devil." The ancient Hebrews thought that when we do wrong we should admit our responsibility and not blame our sins on some evil spirit.

The Hebrews' neighbors also believed that there were two worlds. The one world was perfect—all light, truth and harmony. They maintained that we human beings, on the other hand, are born into another world—one that is part good and part evil, part light and part darkness. The object of our life here is to keep away from the evil and corruption of this world and get to the perfect world of the gods. The two worlds were most commonly called "heaven" and "earth."

Where have you heard of this kind of religion before? Most Christians were raised on it! I do not wish to be disrespectful of parents or ministers, priests and sisters who taught us "to obey God in this life and be happy with Him in the next." They were doing the best they could with what they had received from older generations. But the Hebrews—and therefore Jesus—would have felt the idea that God lives in one world and we live in another is false. For them, there is but one world, God made all of it, and "God saw everything he had made, and indeed, it was very good" (Genesis 1:31).

ABRAHAM'S GOD

Another difference with the Jews might have been put this way by their neighbors: "Those silly Jews think that God knows them by name, that God laughs and cries with them, that God is delighted with them but also can be angry with them. Strangest of all, they believe that when they travel their God goes with them and never leaves them."

The neighbors were right. The faith of the Hebrews in a personal God who loved them was primitive at first, but it has become the most inspired and profound notion of God ever to grace the world.

The great tradition began with a man called Abram, who had a deep faith in the God who called him by a new name—Abraham—and guided him to a new country: "Go from your country and your kindred and your father's house to the land that I will show you. I will make of you a great nation, and I will bless you, and make your name great, so that you will be a blessing" (Genesis 12:1-2).

When God told Abraham to leave his native country, the man packed up all his people, flocks and possessions and did as he was ordered. Later, when God revealed to him that his wife, Sarah, would bear his child even though both of them were old, Abraham believed. There is even a story in the Bible that Abraham was willing to sacrifice his own son, Isaac, if that is what God wanted.

In return for this unquestioning fidelity, God promised Abraham that his descendants would be "as numerous as the stars of heaven and as the sand that is on the seashore" (Genesis 22:17). And so it came to pass. Not only the Jews, but Christians and Muslims as well, look to Abraham as their "founding father."

In the centuries after Abraham, the Hebrews continued to worship the same personal God who had led them into a new land. They thought of God as "father"—not in our sense of the male parent but in the ancient custom of calling the head of the tribe the "father" or "patriarch." This person was responsible for the entire clan. His word was law. When he decided to move, everyone moved. He was the heart and soul of the tribe and held it together. Everything depended on the love, the wisdom, the courage of the patriarch. So when the Hebrew people referred to God as their father, this is what they meant.

Moses' God

In the time of Isaac's son, Jacob, the descendants of Abraham's tribe were suffering a terrible drought. So they went down to Egypt to work as migrant workers. (This was where the famous story of Joseph and his "coat of many colors" comes from.) Egypt, prosperous largely because of the fertile Nile Valley, was empire building at the time.

The Hebrews did well at first in Egypt. Gradually, however, they lost their sense of dignity and freedom. Their increasing numbers threatened the Egyptians, who began to treat them even more harshly, ultimately reducing them to a state of slavery. The Hebrews had forgotten the God of Abraham, but that God had not forgotten them.

A Hebrew child named Moses was born in captivity but was raised in the court of the Pharaoh. One day, the young man Moses saw a soldier mistreating some Hebrew slaves. He got into a fight with the soldier and killed him. Now a criminal, Moses was forced to flee into the desert. There he met a man named Jethro, married his daughter, Zipporah, and settled down to the hard life of tending sheep. It was there in the desert, however, that Moses came into contact with the ancient faith and the God of his forebears.

It happened this way. As he was tending his flock, Moses saw a burning bush—by no means an unusual sight in the blazing heat. But this bush seemed to keep burning without being consumed by the flames. Moses decided to have a look at this strange phenomenon, and as he drew near he heard a voice saying, "Remove the sandals from your feet, for the place on which you are standing is holy ground" (Exodus 3:5). The voice said further, "I am the God of your fathers, the God of Abraham, the God of Isaac, and the God of Jacob" (Exodus 3:6).

The key to this encounter is what God tells Moses to do: "I have observed the misery of my people who are in Egypt; I have heard their cry on account of their taskmasters. Indeed, I know their sufferings, and I have come down to deliver them from the Egyptians, and to bring them up out of that land to a good and broad land, a land flowing with milk and honey" (Exodus 3:7-8).

Notice that once again God is initiating a movement and leading his people to a new and better place. As you can imagine, Moses was stupefied by this command and its enormous challenge. "Who am I that I should go to Pharaoh, and bring the Israelites out of Egypt?" (Exodus 3:11), asks the very reluctant Moses. "I will be with you" (Exodus 3:12), replies God. In desperation, Moses asks who he should say sent him. God replies that Moses should tell them that Yahweh had sent him: "Thus you shall say to the Israelites, 'The Lord, the God of your ancestors, the God of Abraham, the God of Isaac, and the God of Jacob, has sent me to you.'"

Now "Yahweh" means literally "I am who am," or even more exactly "I shall be who I shall be." This became the classic name for the God of Israel, but it is not a proper name at all. It is a way of saying, "Don't ever think you know me or control me."

So Moses does go back to Egypt and eventually leads some (but not all—despite what Cecil B. DeMille would have us believe) of his people out of bondage. This great story of the "Exodus" from Egypt was told over campfires for countless generations among the Hebrews. They told how they passed through what they called "the sea at the end of the world." That was probably a metaphor—a way of saying that God brought them out of the worst predicament in their history, when there was virtually no hope, into freedom and the "promised land." It was an experience they never forgot. God was revealed for all time as the one who would always be with them.

THE CHOSEN PEOPLE

It was to the Hebrews that God gave the Ten Commandments. These were rules for walking together and staying together—instructions on how to relate to God and to one another in peace and harmony. Later on in their history, the Hebrews began to describe God as the creator. By this they did not mean a creator in the sense of the one who makes something out of nothing. The Hebrew mind did not work that way. For them, to create meant to bring order out of disorder, meaning out of chaos.

Through all these centuries, God set up a very special relationship with the Hebrew people that makes them unique in history. This was known as the covenant: "I will take you as my people, and I will be your God" (Exodus 6:7). Thus were the Hebrews given an extraordinary calling or vocation—that of revealing the true God to all nations and of showing the world how a truly godly people should live and act. That is why the Hebrews are called the chosen people and will be so till the end of time.

Prophets and Kings

Once in the promised land, the Hebrews—or Israelites, as they called themselves—experienced many ups and downs. At one point, under King Solomon, they became a major power in the Middle East. Later they suffered disastrous defeats and humiliating captivities. But God never abandoned them, nor did God ever cease to demand that they fulfill their part of the covenant, which was to be God's people, that is, a holy people.

As time went on, God revealed more of the divine nature to the Hebrews through prophets like Ezekiel, Jeremiah and Elijah. These people were spokespersons of the almighty, and they called the Hebrew people back to fidelity to the God of their ancestors. More and more, God was acknowledged to be the God of love and justice. "I desire steadfast love and not sacrifice" (Hosea 6:6), God told them over and over through the prophets. "Cease to do evil, learn to do good; seek justice, rescue the oppressed, defend the orphan, plead for the widow" (Isaiah 1:16-17).

The prophets were quick to condemn the people for their idolatry and injustice. But, in the name of God, they consoled the people by the promise of future salvation. As Isaiah put it: "Sing for joy, O heavens, and exult, O earth; break forth, O mountains, into singing! For the Lord has comforted his people, and will have compassion on his suffering ones" (Isaiah 49:13).

IMAGES OF GOD

It is the God of Abraham, of Moses, of the kings and prophets—whom we Christians worship. We do not worship a God we have made with our hands or invented with our own minds. Rather, we revere the God who is ever present to us, who moves and acts in history—the same Yahweh that was revealed to the Hebrews over many centuries, the same God that Jesus called "Abba" or "Father" or—better yet—"Daddy" or "Papa."

God is always demanding justice, while at the same time offering hope and forgiveness. We shall never understand our God completely. Still—from all we have heard from our spiritual ancestors and have experienced ourselves—we can describe God with one spectacular, fascinating word: passion. God is the one who is passionately in love with us, with our world, and with justice.

We human beings think in images. The Hebrews were forbidden to carve images of God, because once carved they would become static and controllable objects of idolatry. The Hebrews were not forbidden, however, to have images of God in their minds' eyes. Over the centuries, they developed many beautiful images of God. For instance, they pictured God as a dark cloud. Now that may seem strange to us, but for people who lived in the desert, with almost no rainfall, a dark rain cloud approaching was one of the most welcome of sights—a sign of life.

During their stay in the desert, the Hebrews also observed the famous mountain eagle. The mother eagle would take her eaglets at a certain age up to the highest peak. Then she would mount them on her wings and take off. At a certain point, she would cast her young ones into the air. They didn't know how to fly, of course, so they fluttered and began to fall. But each time, the mother eagle would swoop down and catch her young ones on her wings. Then she would return to the peak and repeat the process until the eaglets had learned to fly. The Israelites probably said to each other: "That is just like our God—encouraging us to spread our wings and fly, saving us when we fail, forgiving us, and teaching us to try again until at last we soar freely."

It is the God who was revealed to the ancient Hebrews over many centuries that we Christians believe in. It is that same God of whom Jesus said, "The Father and I are one" (John 10:30).

Questions for Reflection or Discussion

1. How do your images of God compare to those of the ancient Hebrews and of Jesus?

2. What are some of the other gods that you see tempting people today? Which are the most tempting to you?

3. What is the debt that Christians owe to the Jews? What can you do to combat anti-Semitism?

CHAPTER THREE

Jesus the Jew

Did you ever try to picture what Jesus might have looked like? We don't have a definitive answer, but we assume that he looked like most first-century Jewish men. For, like all of us, Jesus was a product of his time and culture. He was so much one of his people that when he first began his public ministry they asked, "Is not this Joseph's son?" (Luke 4:22). This chapter introduces the religious and political world of Jesus.

It was—and still is—God's plan that the faith of the Jewish people is to be a light to the world and the salvation of the Gentiles, that is, of all the other nations of the world. How this has been accomplished is a long, remarkable story—full of suffering as well as glory, of tragedy as well as great promise.

THE BABYLONIAN CAPTIVITY

In 587 BC, the kingdom of Judah, as it was called then, was defeated by Nebuchadnezzar, the king of Babylon. Jerusalem was devastated and Solomon's magnificent temple, one of the wonders of the ancient world, was leveled to the ground. The nobles and warrior chiefs of the Hebrews were executed. Men and women were sold into slavery. Young boys and girls were carried off into captivity in Babylon. All that was left in the land of Israel were old people and a few thousand younger people who had managed to hide from the invaders. New peoples, not Hebrews, were allowed to settle on the land. It was an unmitigated disaster—the beginning of the Diaspora—a word that means the dispersion of the Jewish people throughout the world, which continues to this day.

The cruel practice of carrying off vanquished peoples to foreign lands and selling them into bondage and giving their homeland away to strangers has gone on for centuries—right into our own time. For example, the Soviet Union murdered many people in the Ukraine and shipped countless others to Siberia, giving their property to ethnic Russians, in order to maintain its political control in that country. Even more recently, "ethnic cleansing" took place in Bosnia and Kosovo. Every time this tactic has been used in history, there has been unspeakable suffering. There is no better example of how evil human beings can be than to force others from their homeland and then to take it over for themselves.

THE FAITHFUL ONES

Many of the Hebrew people carried off to Babylon were absorbed into the culture and religion of their captors, but some kept their faith and their identity. They managed to do so by being faithful to the laws and customs of their faith—practices that may seem strange to us today, such as circumcision, purification rituals, dietary laws and the strict observance of the Sabbath. By doing so, the Hebrews were able to recognize that they were still a people hoping to return to their homeland. Wherever Hebrews found one another in exile, they continued to recognize themselves as the chosen people. Fifty years later, Cyrus, the king of Persia, defeated the Babylonians and allowed some of the Hebrew exiles to return. They were small in number but full of enthusiasm. According to the Bible, "The whole assembly together was forty-two thousand three hundred and sixty, besides their male and female slaves" (Ezra 2:64-65).

This small remnant of Israel began the work of rebuilding the temple (the second temple) and the city of Jerusalem and settling the land among the hostile natives who had now lived there for over fifty years. However, the Hebrews continued to live under foreign domination—with the exception of a short period of independence under the Maccabees, which ended about a hundred years before the birth of Christ.

THE TIME OF JESUS

So we come to the first century AD—the time of Jesus. It may be helpful to describe the country and its conditions so that we might understand Jesus more clearly.

Geographically, the land of Israel was some three hundred miles long, from Judea in the south (with Jerusalem as its capital) to Galilee in the north, with Samaria in between. The Hebrew people by this time were called and called themselves Jews—after the name Judah, one of the twelve tribes of Israel.

The Samaritans were a mixed breed of former Jewish inhabitants and foreign settlers. Their religion also was a hybrid. They and the Jewish settlers returning from Babylon were constantly at odds—very much like the Jews and Arabs in present-day Israel.

Politically, the area was ruled and dominated by the Romans—the military and organizational geniuses of their day. They often ruled through local puppets, but everyone knew the real power lay in the hands of Rome.

Culturally, however, the Greeks were dominant. Their language was the one spoken by merchants, traders and educated classes. Everywhere they went, the Greeks established "gymnasiums"—

centers where they spread Greek culture, religion and sports. Many Jews considered them a worse threat than the Romans to Jewish faith and culture. In the gymnasiums, for example, boys and girls played games naked or almost naked, much to the horror of the modest Jewish faithful.

Economically, the situation in Israel at the time of Jesus was bleak. Almost all of the good land was held by large landowners, who lived in the cities and hired overseers to work the land. So people worked as day laborers on the large estates or struggled on small plots. Some worked as fishermen on the Sea of Galilee or on the Mediterranean Sea.

These working poor, however, paid the majority of the taxes. These included a poll tax on the head of every person; a property tax on whatever land you owned; a use tax paid by weavers, carpenters, miners, and other workmen; and, lastly, the temple tax, which supported the vast temple in Jerusalem. The ordinary people considered these taxes excessive and unfair and deeply resented not only the taxes but those who collected them—the corrupt and extortionist "publicans."

Many of the Jewish people wanted to get rid of the Romans by force. Those called "zealots" wanted immediate armed revolt. Others urged compromise and accommodation, but only until such time as they could hope to win a war.

Religiously, Jewish believers at the time of Christ were deeply divided. There were many factions—some small, some rather popular. First were the Sadducees, the priestly party. They were conservative because they were in power and did not want any movement to upset the balance of power between themselves and the Romans. The Romans allowed them to operate the temple—an enormous enterprise with thousands of priests, Levites (the traditional assistants to the priests), attendants and suppliers. The people believed the temple system was riddled with corruption. Still it was the House of God. Or was it?

This was the "second" temple—not the one built by the great Solomon but the one begun after the Babylonian captivity. This temple had been enlarged and magnificently appointed by King Herod the Great. Many asked, however, what right Herod had to have work done on it. He was not a member of the royal family of David. In order to avoid the charge of being an usurper, Herod had married Miriam, a member of the Hasmonean Dynasty (of the time of the Maccabees).

A good number of Jews still thought, however, that the second temple was not really the true dwelling of God. Among them were the Essenes, a sect that thought all of Jewish life at the time was corrupt and hopeless. So they retired from participation in Jewish society and tried to keep themselves pure until God would come to reestablish Israel in all its glory.

Then there were the Pharisees, a large, devout group who were much closer to the people than the Sadducees. The Pharisees were for the most part good, faithful people who believed it was important to maintain the laws and rituals that served to identify Jews to themselves and to others. The Pharisees and the followers of Jesus sometimes disagreed but, in reality, were closer to each other than to the Sadducees. (The serious friction between the Pharisees and the followers of Jesus came much later—maybe fifty years after his death and resurrection.)

THE APPEARANCE OF JESUS

Out of this milieu appeared the man called Jesus. He came from the tiny village of Nazareth in Galilee, the northern province of Israel. His first language was Aramaic—a language akin to both Hebrew and Arabic. (A few years ago, I was in a hospital bed, waiting for a cataract operation. A man occupied the cubicle next to me. He was talking in a foreign language with two visitors. I thought at first it was Hebrew, but I decided it wasn't. So I asked them if they were speaking Arabic. They had recognized me as a priest and asked me, rather amusedly, "Don't you recognize the Lord's own language?" They were speaking Aramaic!)

Jesus almost surely spoke Hebrew as well, having learned it from the local rabbi in order to read the Scriptures. In addition, Jesus' hometown was situated not far from the main trade route between the Mediterranean and the large city of Damascus—so he probably spoke some Greek as well.

The Scriptures tell us that Jesus began his public ministry somewhere around the age of thirty. Where was he and what was he doing until then? Tradition has him working with Joseph as a carpenter, but we really don't know much about those "hidden" years.

One thing is sure, however. Jesus, being fully and completely human, knew nothing when he was born—at least on the human level. He was a "tabula rasa," a clean slate. As Luke says, "Jesus increased in wisdom and in years, and in divine and human favor" (Luke 2:52). So from where did Jesus get his formidable intellectual and spiritual formation?

We do not know. But we can make an educated guess. Likely he went up to Jerusalem or some other urban center, where he studied Scripture, the history of his people, and spirituality—not in a formal school but rather in a place where learned, pious people gathered to hand over their knowledge to the young.

JESUS AND JOHN

We are almost certain that Jesus joined the company of disciples of John the Baptizer. (In fact, the Gospel of Luke tells that they were "cousins," although we do not know for certain that this story was meant to be taken literally.)

John was the most popular and best-known religious figure of his day. Jesus himself would say that John was "more than a prophet" (Matthew 11:9) and that "among those born of women no one has arisen greater than John the Baptist" (Matthew 11:11). John looked at the conditions of Israel at the time and saw change coming—big, radical change. God, he believed, would intervene in Israel's history once again, since the situation could not go on as it was. John warned people about their sins, their apathy, their arrogance and the punishment to come.

John often preached at the spot in the River Jordan where the river was narrow. He exhorted people to acknowledge their sins—not just their individual sins but more importantly their collective sins as a people—of infidelity and injustice. Then John baptized them by having them enter the river on one side and emerge on the other.

Evidently, Jesus walked and worked with John for a good space of time, perhaps for several years—listening, praying, meditating on what the "great day of the Lord"—John's favorite theme—meant to himself. Then suddenly John was thrown in jail by King Herod Antipas. His career over, John heard about the new activity of Jesus.

So he sent messengers from his prison to ask Jesus what he was up to. Jesus replied, "Go and tell John what you hear and see: the blind receive their sight, the lame walk, the lepers are cleansed, the deaf hear, the dead are raised, and the poor have good news brought to them" (Matthew 11:4-5).

In his answer, Jesus was using a text of the prophet Isaiah, a passage that would have been well known to both John and Jesus. Jesus was saying that "the reign of God"—for which John and all Jews waited—had begun in the person of Jesus himself. Then Jesus added: "Blessed is anyone who takes no offense at me" (Matthew 11:6). In other words, Jesus expected John to be surprised by Jesus' proclamation and, maybe, even incredulous.

Jesus was saying that the Messiah, the long-awaited one who would deliver Israel from its woes, had appeared—and that he himself was the one!

THE KINGDOM OF GOD

From the beginning, Jesus announced that the reign of God was near, so near it had actually begun. There is no word in English that can adequately translate the grandeur and depth of the reality Jesus called "the reign of God," "the kingdom of God," and "the kingdom of heaven."

You and I don't especially like kings and queens these days, nor are we pleased with the idea of reigns or kingdoms. Some try to translate the term as "God's breaking through" or "God's love ruling the world," but these words do not do the job either. So let us stick with "kingdom" or "reign"—even though these words may have unpleasant connotations and don't begin to express the great mystery behind them.

We, in our time, also make a mistake when we think of the kingdom of God as the place where the good go after they die, a place we call "heaven." This idea would have made little sense to first-century Jews—our parents in the faith and the people from whom Jesus emerged.

What did the Jews—and therefore Jesus—believe about the reign of God?

First, they believed that they still lived in exile because of their sins. Some of them had returned to their ancient homeland, but since the land wasn't really theirs they were still, in a sense, in exile. One sign of the coming of the reign of God would be when God publicly forgave their sins as a nation: "I will restore the fortunes of Judah and the fortunes of Israel, and rebuild them as they were at first. I will cleanse them from all the guilt of their sin against me, and I will forgive all the guilt of their sin and rebellion against me" (Jeremiah 33:7-8).

Second, the Jews believed that God would return to Israel to dwell in the temple at Jerusalem, just as in the glory days of Israel.

Third, they thought that those who had given their lives for the sake of the kingdom would rise from their graves and come to life again.

Fourth, they expected that the land would be restored to the people and sovereignty to the nation.

Fifth, they looked forward to an outpouring of the spirit of God on all the people—a new and abundant spirit of love, forgiveness, compassion, openness, justice.

Lastly, the Jews believed that all nations would come to Jerusalem to learn about the one true God and to learn what it means to live as a holy people: "In days to come, the mountain of the Lord's house shall be established as the highest of the mountains, and shall be raised above the hills; all the nations shall stream toward it" (Isaiah 2:2).

Jesus' Understanding of the Kingdom

It was this vision and expectation of the kingdom that Jesus received from his elders—especially from those steeped in the wisdom of the law and the prophets. It may well have taken him years of prayer, study and dialogue—as well as his discipleship under John the Baptizer—to figure out his role in the coming of the kingdom of God. He had to see clearly God's will before he moved. And when he did see it, he accepted the coming of God's reign with all his heart and soul.

But Jesus also courageously and surprisingly reinterpreted the Jewish vision of the kingdom of God in a radical manner. He claimed publicly that God had in fact come to dwell among God's people not in the temple at Jerusalem but in Jesus himself—the true and everlasting temple of God—and in each and every one of us, whom he called "children of God."

In addition, recognizing that his own people—the Jews—were in danger of turning inward on themselves, Jesus eventually came to understand that he must share his vision of the kingdom of God with everyone. As the holy man Simeon proclaimed when Mary and Joseph first presented their infant son in the temple, "My eyes have seen your salvation, which you have prepared in the presence of all peoples, a light for revelation to the Gentiles and for glory to your people Israel" (Luke 2:32).

Questions for Reflection or Discussion

1. What about the time and culture of Jesus fascinates you? Why?

2. Imagine a conversation between Jesus and John the Baptizer before John was arrested. What might they have been worried about? What things would have excited them or given them hope?

3. What are some other words or images that we could use to describe the reality that Jesus called "the kingdom of God"?

CHAPTER FOUR

Jesus the Parable Teller

Did you ever wonder what Jesus meant by some of his sayings and parables? Do some of them seem hopelessly optimistic or impossible to follow? The key to understanding the message of Jesus is to learn what he meant when he said, "The kingdom of God has come near" (Mark 1:15). This chapter leads us through some of the best-known teachings of Jesus.

No one in all of history has fascinated people more than Jesus of Nazareth. Countless people have followed him as their savior. Innumerable books, plays, movies have been made about him. He is probably the subject of more art than any other figure in humankind (with the possible exception of his mother). Why this fascination? I believe it is because Jesus himself was fascinated by something and was able to fascinate others. By what? By the idea of the kingdom of God.

Jesus preached that kingdom, he lived it, and he died for it. It was the theme of his preaching, day in and day out. In the very first chapter of the oldest of the four gospels we hear how, after John the Baptizer was arrested, "Jesus came to Galilee, proclaiming the good news of God, and saying, 'The time is fulfilled, and the kingdom of God has come near; repent, and believe in the good news'" (Mark 1:14-15).

We hear the same in the Gospel of Matthew: "From that time Jesus began to proclaim, 'Repent, for the kingdom of heaven has come near'" (Matthew 4:17). Luke also has Jesus saying urgently, "I must proclaim the good news of the kingdom of God to the other cities also; for I was sent for this purpose" (Luke 4:43).

Matthew, in fact, gives us a sentence that is the topical sentence of the gospels, the heart of Jesus' message: "Strive first for the kingdom of God and his righteousness, and all these things will be given to you as well" (Matthew 6:33).

WHAT DID JESUS MEAN?

What did Jesus mean by the "reign" or the "kingdom" of God? Jesus, like all believing Jews of his time, held that the current situation of his people would not be God's last word on Israel—nor on the rest of the world for that matter. Jesus believed that God was faithful and that one day the power of God would break through the intransigence of the people to reconstruct Israel.

Then a new age would begin. There would occur a total transformation of reality—not merely a transformation of the inner person but a radical change in all of society. When God (whom Jesus knew as a loving father) broke through, there would be a huge change in relationships: people would believe and trust in God as never before, and fellowship and reconciliation between human beings would become the norm.

This "salvation" would not be brought on by human ingenuity—such as was envisioned by Thomas More's Utopia or Lyndon Johnson's Great Society—but rather by grace, which was God's free gift. Jesus warned that the kingdom would never be hastened by obedience to the law, nor could it be accomplished by violence.

What would the kingdom of God look like? Like everything else divine, it would be invisible and mysterious. But Jesus felt that the signs of the kingdom and its effects among human beings would be abundantly clear. The kingdom would be inclusive—no one, no one at all, would be left out. It would be a place of forgiveness, compassion, equality, fairness, justice.

In fact, Jesus announced, the long awaited reign of God had already started! It existed in Jesus' very person and in those who believed as he did.

PARABLES OF THE KINGDOM

Jesus proclaimed the arrival of the kingdom day after day. His method of preaching was striking. He taught by telling a type of story almost unique to himself that we now call parables. It is important that we know exactly what a parable is, because it represents the main teaching device of Jesus. A parable, by definition, is "a narrative fiction that refers to a symbol." It is neither an allegory nor a fable, but rather a made-up story that points beyond itself to something else. A parable is meant to be told or even performed. It is designed to be provocative, surprising and mind-opening. It seeks to boggle the mind.

All of Jesus' parables point to some aspect of the wonderful new reality God was ushering in. It is a mistake to take one of Jesus' parables and try to interpret it without reference to the kingdom of God. Let's take some of Jesus' more famous parables and try to discern from them what Jesus meant by the kingdom of God.

For example, he said that the kingdom of God "is like a grain of mustard seed, which, when sown upon the ground, is the smallest of all the seeds on earth; yet when it is sown it grows up and becomes the greatest of all shrubs, and puts forth branches, so that the birds of the air can make nests in its shade" (Mark 4:31-32).

In this parable, Jesus was talking to the handful of followers who became the beginning of the greatest religious movement in history. They, however, regarded themselves as unimportant, and they knew that they were few. So Jesus uses the mustard seed as an example. Not only is the seed small, but the mustard tree itself was considered useless and pernicious to other trees. It was even forbidden to plant a mustard tree in a garden in the time of Jesus.

Yet here Jesus was saying that the mustard tree is "the greatest of all shrubs." Now do you get the meaning? It's provocative and surprising: not only will the kingdom come out of modest beginnings, but the kingdom will redefine "greatness" itself!

THE KINGDOM AS YEAST

Another time, Jesus says, "To what shall I compare the kingdom of God? It is like yeast that a woman took and mixed in with three measures of flour until all of it was leavened" (Luke 13:20-21). What does this little simile mean?

First, three measures of flour is a huge amount—enough to make maybe fifty pounds of bread. Second, there was no nice packaged yeast as we know it in Jesus' time. People took a piece of stale bread and put it in a dark corner until it was moldy. It was the mold that served as leaven.

So Jesus was saying that just as something smelly and corrupt could produce a vast amount of bread, so too would common, sinful folk—his followers—transform not only Israel but the entire world as well.

For Jesus, this belief in God's ability to bring about a whole new world of peace and love and justice is worth more than anything else in life. So he likened the vision of the reign of God to "a merchant in search of fine pearls; on finding one pearl of great value, he went and sold all that he had and bought it" (Matthew 13:45-46) or to "a treasure hidden in a field, which someone found and hid; then in his joy he goes and sells all that he has and buys that field"(Matthew 13:44).

THE PRODIGAL SON

Perhaps Jesus' greatest parable of the kingdom is the one we call "The Prodigal Son," although really we should call it "The Indulgent Father." Even if we were to lose all the rest of the gospels, I submit we could reconstruct Jesus' vision of God and the kingdom through this one lovely story.

The younger son is mean, wild and selfish. He asks his father for his share of the estate now. For the Jews, this would have been the same as wishing his father dead in order to get his hands on the money. The insult to and rejection of the old man must have shocked people listening to that story.

Then the son goes off to a foreign country (imagine the hearers thinking of a young Jew forsaking his own family and country and faith). There he spends all he has on wild living. Finally, the money runs out, his health deteriorates, and he is starving–fighting with pigs for a husk of corn. Again, Jesus' listeners couldn't possibly have imagined a more degraded, shameful condition.

Eventually, the boy comes to himself and says, "I will get up and go to my father, and I will say to him, 'Father, I have sinned against heaven and before you; I am no longer worthy to be called your son; treat me like one of your hired hands'" (Luke 15:18-19).

So he heads home. The father has been looking down the road every day for a glimpse of his lost son. When he sees him coming down the road, he runs to meet him and throws his arms around the boy and hugs him. The son starts his well-rehearsed story (somehow we question whether he is sincere), but the father forgives him without conditions.

Then another dark shadow enters the story. The older son is bitter and resentful and doesn't want to forgive and reclaim his wayward brother. The older son stands for all of us, who want ourselves to be loved and forgiven but are not too sure about others.

This parable presents a truly remarkable picture of God. God is the one who forgives always, unconditionally—no ifs, ands, or buts. (The Dutch painter Rembrandt was inspired to paint the scene on canvas. There in the light is a richly dressed old man embracing a younger man clothed in rags. We see clearly the old man's hands clutching the back of his son. One hand is a man's, the other is a woman's. Rembrandt is saying that God's love is both strong and tender, both masculine and feminine. Many say that painting, now hanging in the Hermitage Museum in St. Petersburg, Russia, is the finest painting of all times. To my mind, this would be fitting, because that parable is the best of all the parables.)

But what does the parable mean? Remember that every one of Jesus' parables refers to the kingdom of God. The older son doesn't want to forgive, but Jesus is saying that the kingdom means forgiveness. We must be like God and forgive or we cannot enter God's kingdom. There are no exceptions to this forgiveness, even for the worst of sinners, the cruelest of criminals, or even the dumbest of children.

When we pray "Your kingdom come" we also ask God to "forgive us...as we also have forgiven" (Matthew 6:12).

THE LABORERS IN THE FIELD

Let us take one more parable about the kingdom, that of the day laborers in the field.

You remember the story of how the owner of the vineyard hired workers at 6 a.m. to work on his farm. Then he saw men at 9 a.m. who had no work yet so he hired them also. The same thing happened at noon, at 3 p.m. and even at 5 p.m.

The owner paid the last workers first, a full day's pay. He then paid all the rest—ending with those who had started at 6 a.m. Much to their surprise, they were paid the same wage as those who had worked only a couple of hours. They grumbled that it wasn't fair. The owner replied, "Friend, I am doing you no wrong; did you not agree with me for the usual daily wage? Take what belongs to you and go; I choose to give to this last the same as I give to you. Am I not allowed to do what I choose with what belongs to me? Or are you envious because I am generous?" (Matthew 20:13-15).

What does this strange, yet very human, story tell us about the kingdom? It says that God is the real ruler of our world. God does what God wishes when God chooses to do so. Or, as the Hebrew Scriptures put it, "For my thoughts are not your thoughts, nor are your ways my ways, says the Lord" (Isaiah 55:8).

Think of it this way. If you went out to pick laborers for some work in your factory, whom would you choose? The weakest, the least experienced, the crippled, those who are hung over? Of course not. You would choose the fittest, the strongest, the most capable. And if you went back to the labor pool, late in the day, who would most likely be left? Probably the least employable. Yet in this parable the owner (that is, God) gives the weakest a break because, incomprehensible as it might be, that's the way God does things.

Many years ago I prepared a man in prison for his death. He had been tried and convicted of murder and sentenced to be executed in the electric chair. I heard his confession and absolved him. As far as I could tell he was sincere in his sorrow. The story of my hearing his confession appeared in the daily papers, and I was mentioned by name. Much to my amazement and sorrow, people called me to ask why I had given the man absolution. "The rest of us live all our lives obeying the laws of God and trying our best to be good," they said. "But you forgave a murderer who has led a terrible life, and then he could go straight to heaven. It just isn't fair!"

Those callers would never understand this parable. They were Christians, in name anyway, but they were far from the kingdom of God.

THE KEYS TO THE KINGDOM

The experts in sacred Scripture tell us that the teachings of Jesus were handed down by word of mouth for some forty or fifty years before the gospels were written. Because they were in the form of easily remembered stories and because they all had his distinctive style, the parables are probably the nearest thing we have to the actual words of Jesus himself.

So each time we read them we get a new insight into the mind and heart of Jesus.

After sharing several parables with his disciples one day, Jesus asked them, "Have you understood all this?" (Matthew 13:51). They said that they had, and Jesus told them, "Therefore every scribe (a scribe is an expert in Mosaic Law) who has been trained for the kingdom of heaven is like the master of a household who brings out of his treasure what is new and what is old" (Matthew 13:52). Let us hope that the parables can help us to bring out the new and the old of the treasure that so fascinated Jesus—the vision of kingdom of God.

Questions for Reflection or Discussion

1. What is your favorite parable from the gospels? Why do you like it or what does it say to you?

2. What are some times in your life when you have been forgiven or forgiven others? What was difficult about giving or receiving forgiveness?

3. If and when the kingdom truly and completely "comes," how do you think things will be different? What would the world be like? What is preventing that from happening now?

CHAPTER 5

Jesus the Healer

How many times have you prayed that you or someone you love be healed? What happened? People in the first century prayed in much the same way, but suddenly Jesus was among them: "And all in the crowd were trying to touch him, for power came out from him and healed all of them" (Luke 6:19). This chapter explores the unique kind of healing that Jesus performed and how it was connected to his idea of the kingdom of God.

Another reason that people throughout the ages have been fascinated with Jesus is that he was a healer. In his time, there were a few who practiced a very primitive type of medicine. But however inadequate their skill, they still served only the rich. There were also many quacks and magicians around who claimed to heal people, but they always asked for money and their cures were gradual, if they worked at all.

So most people in Israel were desperate when they had to face a serious illness. Then along came Jesus, and they flocked to him. Why did they believe in him as a healer? First, because he was manifestly a holy man who loved and served the poor. Ancient people of every culture have always associated God's healing power with holy men and women. Secondly, because they saw what Jesus did. When John the Baptizer's messengers asked, "Are you the one who is to come, or are we to wait for another?" (Matthew 11:3), Jesus answered, "Go and tell John what you hear and see: the blind receive their sight, the lame walk, the lepers are cleansed, the deaf hear, the dead are raised, and the poor have good news brought to them" (Matthew 11:4-5).

A man born blind was able to see after Jesus put some earth and spittle on his eyes. A woman with constant menstrual flow was cured by touching the hem of Jesus' cloak. The daughter of the centurion was cured while Jesus was still a long way off. The only son of a widow was raised while lying on a funeral bier being carried to the cemetery. No wonder the people were impressed by Jesus. These were real miracles!

THE MIRACLE WORKER

By definition, a miracle is a startling or extraordinary event that is perceivable by any fair-minded observer, an event that finds no reasonable explanation in human abilities or other known forces of our world, an event that is the result of a special act of God that accomplishes what no human power can. There are many people today who deny altogether the miracles performed by Jesus. They say Jesus was a good man and a great teacher but that the miracles ascribed to him never happened because they can't happen.

The people in the time of Jesus, however, saw and believed in the miracles Jesus performed. Jesus himself evidently believed in the power God gave him. If, therefore, you throw out the miracles you gut the gospels and you're forced to discard the whole story of Jesus.

Why did Jesus work these wonders? The most obvious answer is that he was kind and compassionate. He shared the compassion of the God of love, the God whom Jesus called "Father," for whom every human being is someone precious. But there is another answer, a deeper one, to why Jesus worked miracles. It was held by many at that time that only the holy, the bright, the best, the wholesome would enter the new age—the reign of God—when finally it came. Sinners, especially publicans (or tax collectors) and prostitutes, would be excluded as well as all the so-called "misfits" of society—including those with serious illnesses or disabilities. (We still see this attitude today in many supposed "Christians.")

With his miracles, Jesus was proclaiming that the great day of the coming of the kingdom had already dawned. There was only one thing Jesus found he could not do and that was heal a person who did not believe. "Go now," he often said after healing a person. "Your faith has saved you." People who were sick had to believe not only in Jesus, but in the God who loved them and promised them a whole new future. In Jesus' eyes, worse than any illness, disability, poverty, or misfortune is to give up hope and accept the present as God's "last word" on the way things should be.

Matthew says Jesus cured "all" the sick: "Jesus went about all the cities and villages, teaching in their synagogues, and proclaiming the good news of the kingdom, and curing every disease and every sickness. When he saw the crowds, he had compassion for them, because they were harassed and troubled, like sheep without a shepherd" (Matthew 9:35-36).

Isn't it an exaggeration that Jesus cured "everybody"? If that were true, wouldn't he have been overwhelmed by the whole country, and eventually by the whole world? Yes, if we are to take the idea of healing in its most narrow sense. But couldn't Matthew mean that all who saw the wonders worked by this kind and holy man were healed of their hopelessness? Wouldn't they have exclaimed there is always hope as long as there is someone around like Jesus? Wouldn't they have realized and rejoiced in the proof provided by Jesus that God has not abandoned us?

CASTING OUT DEMONS

Among the healing gifts of Jesus was that of expelling demons from people. This is a subject that puzzles and confuses modern people, but belief in demonic possession was common in his time and culture.

What is meant by "possession by the devil"? Our usual image is of a little girl physically dominated by a fiercely evil spirit, but this image comes from a Hollywood movie, *The Exorcist*. I have served as a priest for fifty years and I have never seen anything close to that. Furthermore, I have known priests and ministers, hundreds of them, and I have never encountered even one who has been confronted by a "real devil" within a human being. I'm not saying it's not possible, merely that I have not seen it nor have I known someone who has.

The question, then, rises naturally: why was diabolical possession so common in the time of Jesus and so rare, even non-existent, in our day? This may be a clue: the Hebrew words for the devil mean "the one who lies, the one who divides, the one who deceives." That means that Satan is the exact opposite of God–the one who is truth, the one who is faithful, the one who reconciles people.

The people of that time, including Jesus himself, would have seen the same things we do, but they might have understood them differently. For example, they observed the frightening and ugly phenomenon of a man who is extremely disordered: "In the synagogue there was a man who had the spirit of an unclean demon" (Luke 4:33). We might describe him as a having a severe schizophrenia because we are aware of the effects of mental illness. The people of the time of Jesus were not stupid, but they had no awareness of the idea of mental or psychological conditions. So they would have externalized the phenomenon, saying that it was a disorder caused by the divider, the devil himself.

The situation would have scared them, since they had no idea how to deal with it. (Nor do we today, many times–just look at how we treat the homeless.) Jesus, filled with the power of God, was able somehow to heal the man, saying, "Be silent, and come out of him!" (Luke 4:35). We don't understand what happened, but "when the demon had thrown him down before them, he came out of him without having done him any harm" (Luke 4:35). Somehow Jesus was able to affect the man in such a way as to make him whole. "With authority and power he commands the unclean spirits, and out they come!" (Luke 4:36), the people exclaimed.

I said that diabolical possession is not common in our age, but I would like to modify that statement, maybe even correct it. How many of us have a severe problem of addiction? Addiction to alcohol, to drugs, to gambling, to eating, to sex, even to work? A person can be completely dominated by the affliction. One of the signs of addiction is a change in personality. Addicts become another kind of human being—not their true selves but rather a parody of themselves. We used to think it was a moral problem—that all the addict had to do was admit the behavior was wrong and resolve not to do it again. But now we know better. The afflicted person has to acknowledge the problem and his or her powerless to correct it, plead for and rely on the help of God, and often join a group that is seeking healing. This is the core of the famous "twelve-step" program first developed by Alcoholics Anonymous.

Maybe Jesus accomplished this same kind of healing instantly, "by the finger of God," as he himself put it: "If it is by the finger of God that I cast out the demons, then the kingdom of God has come to you" (Luke 11:20).

Healing the "Sin-Sick Soul"

Jesus cured diseased bodies and disturbed minds, but—greatest of all—he healed afflicted souls by forgiving their sins. There is no greater tragedy than sin. Some things we do shame us so badly we find it almost impossible to live with them. Other things we don't do—such as offering a kind word or deed when it is needed—also cause us lingering regret. We hurt people close to us, and then we can find no way to make it up to them. Bitterly, we cry, "It's too late."

Jesus came to heal our "sin-sick souls" as the lovely black spiritual goes. He forgave prostitutes, the thief on the cross next to him, the woman caught in adultery. You remember that story. She was dragged before Jesus and the crowd—all men, you notice—said, "Teacher, this woman was caught in the very act of committing adultery. Now in the law Moses commanded us to stone such women. Now what do you say?" (John 8:4-5).

Jesus bends over to write on the ground. It may well be that he was evoking the memory of God writing the Ten Commandments in the stone tablets. But Jesus is writing a different commandment: forgive others as God forgives you. "Let anyone among you who is without sin be the first to throw a stone at her" (John 8:7), he says.

They refuse, dropping their stones and shrinking away, the eldest first, then the young men, finally the last teenage boy. There are two interpretations of this. One is that the older men realize before the younger how much they have sinned. The other is that the older men refuse to forgive first, since they are so set in their ways, and the younger men follow their example.

Either way, when Jesus straightens up, he and the woman are alone: "'Has no one condemned you?' he asks. 'No one, sir,' she replies. 'Neither do I condemn you,' he says. 'Go your way, and from now on do not sin again'" (John 8:10-11). Notice that Jesus did not scold the woman. He asked no questions about why she had sinned, he set no conditions on God's forgiveness. His only command is that she sin no more. As far as Jesus is concerned, she has been made whole and clean again—as good and as holy as anyone in town.

Another story of forgiveness is about Zacchaeus the tax collector. Tax collectors of the time were collecting taxes for the Romans. When people couldn't pay on time, the tax collectors added penalties, which they got to keep for themselves. In effect, they were giving very high interest or "juice" loans to people, just like in today's Mafia movies. Because of this, tax collectors were despised and ostracized by their own people. What they did was unforgivable.

Zacchaeus, a short fellow, climbed up into a sycamore tree in order to get a look at the famous healer Jesus. Jesus spies him there and says, "Zacchaeus, hurry and come down; for I must stay at your house today" (Luke 19:5). You can imagine the smile on the face of Jesus, the amazement in the eyes of Zacchaeus, and the grumbling of everybody else: "He has gone to be the guest of one who is a sinner" (Luke 19:7). We don't go to supper at the house of an enemy, only of a friend, but Zacchaeus was already forgiven, even before he had a chance to say he was sorry. Jesus said, "Today salvation has come to this house, because he too is a son of Abraham. For the Son of Man came to seek out and to save the lost" (Luke 19:9-10). As a result of Jesus' action, Zacchaeus changes his life—promising to give half of his possessions to the poor and to repay anyone he has cheated four-fold. Such is the healing power of forgiveness.

Finally, there is the story of the paralyzed man on the stretcher. I like to imagine this man and his companions as the reprobates of the town. The man is paying the price of a lifetime of excessive debauchery—he is paralyzed and cannot walk. His buddies can't get anywhere near Jesus to get help for their friend, so they cleverly climb up on the roof of the house where Jesus is staying. They remove some roof tiles and lower the paralyzed man down through the roof.

The rest of the people in the room looking up at the descending body are surprised and many are angry at the impertinence, but not Jesus. I imagine that he admires the men's loyalty to their friend and the paralytic's determination to be healed. Before anyone can say anything, however, Jesus says, "Friend, your sins are forgiven you" (Luke 5:20). Now, this is a strange starting place for this conversation, but the scribes and the Pharisees bite immediately on Jesus' hook: "Who can forgive sins but God alone?" (Luke 5:21).

Who indeed? Jesus delivers his punch line: "Why do you raise such questions in your hearts? Which is easier to say, 'Your sins are forgiven you,' or to say, 'Stand up and walk'? But so you may know that the Son of Man has authority on earth to forgive sins"—he said to the one who was paralyzed—"I say to you, stand up and take your bed and go to your home" (Luke 5:22-24).

Jesus is announcing that the coming of the kingdom begins by forgiving sins. This was risky, as we will see later, because the Jewish establishment said that people must go through the ritual purifications in the temple at Jerusalem. But Jesus did away with such rites by forgiving sins himself and empowering his disciples to do so also: "If you forgive the sins of any, they are forgiven them" (John 20:23).

"Your Kingdom Come"

The wonders performed by Jesus proclaimed the mercy of God to all—the sick and the sound, the clean and the unclean, the sinner and the saint. All were forgiven, all were paid the same wages. No believer, no matter what his or her condition, would be denied entrance to the kingdom of God. The so-called good, healthy, law-abiding people have a choice: either accept all the "misfits" or be denied entrance to the kingdom themselves.

When the disciples asked Jesus to teach them to pray, he not only taught them how to pray, but more importantly what to pray for. The center of what we call the Our Father or Lord's Prayer are these words: "Your kingdom come" and "forgive us our sins" (Luke 11:2, 4).

Questions for Reflection or Discussion

1. Describe a time when you or someone you love were "healed." Did forgiveness play a part in the healing? How?

2. Which is your favorite healing story in the gospels. Why?

3. In what ways do you heal others in your life? How can you begin to do a better job of it?

CHAPTER SIX

Jesus Is Condemned

Have you ever wondered what exactly Jesus did or what threat he was to the establishment of his time that led to his condemnation and terrible death on the cross? Jesus' passion was real. He felt the pain and experienced the sense of failure just as we would. "My God, my God, why have you forsaken me?" (Matthew 27:46), he cried from the cross. This chapter tries to explain the rejection of Jesus by so many of his contemporaries and how it was directly connected to his teaching on the kingdom of God.

We have seen that the kingdom of God was the message of the preaching of Jesus. Moreover, it was the dream he lived and his undying hope. Did he think the kingdom was already present or that it was yet to come? The answer is both.

The Pharisees asked Jesus when the kingdom of God was coming, and he answered, "The kingdom of God is not coming with things that can be observed; nor will they say, 'Look, here it is!' or 'There it is!' For, in fact, the kingdom of God is among you" (Luke 17:20-21). Jesus also told his disciples how fortunate they were to see the dawning of the kingdom: "Blessed are the eyes that see what you see! For I tell you that many prophets and kings desired to see what you see, but did not see it, and to hear what you hear, but did not hear it" (Luke 10:23-24).

Yet at the same time Jesus sees the kingdom as something coming in the future: "He said to them: 'I have eagerly desired to eat this Passover with you before I suffer; for I tell you, I will not eat it until it is fulfilled in the kingdom of God.' Then he took a cup, and after giving thanks he said, 'Take this and divide it among yourselves; for I tell you that from now on I will not drink of the fruit of the vine until the kingdom of God comes'" (Luke 22:14-19).

For Jesus, then, the kingdom is present when people acknowledge that God is already among those people who love as God loves—excluding no one, with fairness and compassion, with no hatred, vengeance or discrimination. And yet that kingdom is not complete until it is entered into and embraced by everyone—until the entire human race is at peace and in love with God and with one another.

THE REJECTION OF JESUS

Who would oppose this vision of human life? What about it threatened people? Why didn't everyone become his disciple? How did Jesus develop so many deadly enemies so quickly?

Jesus plainly considered resisting the kingdom or standing in its way the greatest sin, and there were certainly many who did that. First were the rich and powerful, because they were satisfied with the way things were. "Woe to you who are rich," he said, "for you have received your consolation" (Luke 6:24). He also said, "It is easier for a camel to go through the eye of a needle than for someone who is rich to enter the kingdom of God" (Mark 10:25). This does not mean that people who are well off cannot enter the kingdom—many, such as Joseph of Arimathea and many others throughout the centuries, have obviously done so. But it does mean that it is extremely difficult to get beyond our love for money and material possessions to embrace God's way.

Jesus reserved his harshest criticism, however, for the official teachers of Israel, who made all kinds of rules and laws and imposed impossible burdens on people, but never gave them hope for change: "Woe to you, scribes and Pharisees, hypocrites! For you lock people out of the kingdom of heaven. For you do not go in yourselves, and when others are going in, you stop them" (Matthew 23:13).

Such words are, of course, designed to make enemies, but Jesus never backed down—no matter what the consequences. He would defend his dream of the way the world should be, even if it cost him his life.

What hurt Jesus most, however, was the defection of his friends and followers. The Gospel of John tells us that at a certain point many of Jesus' followers began to walk away from him. With sorrow he watched them go. He turned to his very best friends, the apostles, and asked, "Do you also wish to go away?" (John 6:67). Simon Peter answered for all of them: "Lord, to whom can we go? You have the words of eternal life" (John 6:68).

JESUS' DIFFERING VIEW OF THE KINGDOM OF GOD

From all accounts, Jesus was a gentle, loving man. How do we account for the fierce opposition to him from the leaders of his own people? How in the world do we explain the rejection he experienced from his own followers?

I think it was because of Jesus' message of the kingdom of God. In one way, this was a vision he shared with all thoughtful, believing Jews of the time. But Jesus was radically reinterpreting that dream.

First, the Jews believed that God would one day return to Israel and dwell again in the temple. Jesus proclaimed that God had returned and dwelt in him—not in the temple at Jerusalem. He was the new temple, not made by the hands of men but by God. One of the charges leveled against Jesus before the high priest was that he made himself greater than the temple. He was charged with claiming, "I will destroy this temple that is made with hands, and in three days I will build another, not made with hands" (Mark 14:58).

Second, the people believed that accompanying the coming of the kingdom would be a sign from God proclaiming the forgiveness of sins. Jesus declared that he was that sign. He forgave sins and commanded his followers to forgive sins. His death on the cross would become the public, universal, timeless sign from God that all sin has been conquered.

With these two extraordinary claims, Jesus undermined the very establishment of the religion of his day, especially of the Sadducees, who maintained a monopoly on worship and the forgiveness of sins until Jesus came along. There seem to be no doubt that, at least to some degree, Jesus opposed the temple and what it stood for. Charging "you have made it a den of robbers" (Mark 11:17), he staged a public protest within the temple precincts, and with that act he precipitated the final crisis and signed his own death warrant. There is even some speculation that Judas betrayed Jesus precisely over the issue of substituting a communal meal (the Eucharist) for the animal sacrifices of the temple as the main or ordinary form of worship.

A third difference in Jesus' understanding of the kingdom had to do with the idea of resurrection. Part of the Jewish expectation of the coming of the kingdom was that those who had died serving the kingdom would rise from the dead. Jesus predicted that he himself would be the first to rise from the dead, although we shall see that resurrection for him would mean something very different from what the Jews of his time had in mind. "I am the resurrection and the life. Those who believe in me, even though they die, will live, and everyone who lives and believes in me will never die" (John 11:25-26), he said.

The fourth and perhaps the most telling difference between Jesus and the people of his time was their expectation that when the kingdom of God came, the foreign powers that were oppressing Israel would be soundly defeated and expelled from the land. Sovereignty would return to Israel and the land to its people. Then all the nations of the world would come to Jerusalem to worship the one true God. The spirit of God would come to the Israelites, making them once again a holy and just people, an example of holiness to all the nations of the earth.

Clearly, Jesus thought that Israel was turning in on itself with this concept of the kingdom. He advocated a policy of inclusion in the kingdom: all the misfits, all the foreigners, all the sinners would be welcome. Further, he objected to violence and war as a means of spreading the good news. "My kingdom is not from this world. If my kingdom were from this world, my followers would be fighting to keep me from being handed over" (John 18:36), he told Pontius Pilate. And when his followers did try to fight, he told them, "Put your sword back into its place; for all who take the sword will perish by the sword" (Matthew 26:52).

Jesus, a true prophet, warned his people that if they fought the Romans on the Romans' terms—that is to say, military action—they would be destroyed in the process. Jesus tried to warn them—and us, as well—that pursuing freedom through violence would lead to disaster. Some think that Jesus predicted the end of the world, but there is no reason why Jesus would have believed that God was going to destroy the world, which is God's own creation and home. Jesus was not foretelling the end of the world of space and time, but rather, in a very dramatic fashion, the end of the world as he knew it, the end of Israel as it was in those days: "For there will be great distress on the earth and wrath against this people; they will fall by the edge of the sword and be taken away as captives among all nations; and Jerusalem will be trampled on by the Gentiles, until the times of the Gentiles are fulfilled" (Luke 21:23-24).

Jesus' statement would be fulfilled only thirty-five years later when the Roman armies laid siege to Jerusalem and then utterly destroyed both the temple and the city itself. Most of the inhabitants of the land were scattered around the world. The opposition of Jesus to war and violence as the way to build the kingdom of God was clearly vindicated.

Finally, while the Jews believed that when the spirit of God came upon the nation all the peoples of the earth would flock to Israel to see God's justice being lived out, Jesus saw the kingdom very differently. He urged his followers to go out to the far corners of the earth, announcing his vision of the good news of the kingdom: "Go therefore and make disciples of all nations, baptizing them in the name of the Father and of the Son and of the Holy Spirit, and teaching them to obey everything that I have commanded you" (Matthew 28:19-20).

THE SUFFERING SERVANT

Many opposed Jesus because they simply could not agree with his reinterpretation of the kingdom of God. Even some of his own followers walked away because they both expected and wanted the kingdom to mean a glorious victory over Israel's enemies and a place of prestige and power for them in the new order.

As the opposition to Jesus' message grew and the number of defections increased, he became more and more convinced that God's victory over sin and slavery would be won not by force but rather by his own defeat and failure, his own suffering and death. To us, this is a strange way to think about victory and salvation. But it was not so strange for a believing Jew such as Jesus.

There was a strong tradition among the chosen people that the savior would be what the prophet Isaiah called the "suffering servant." The entire fifty-third chapter of the book of Isaiah speaks of this: "He was despised and rejected by others; a man of suffering and acquainted with infirmity, and as one from whom others hide their faces he was despised, and we held him of no account. Surely he has born our infirmities and carried our diseases; yet we accounted him stricken, struck down by God, and afflicted. But he was wounded for our transgressions, crushed for our iniquities; upon him was the punishment that made us whole, and by his bruises we are healed" (Isaiah 53:3-5).

This tradition declared that Israel itself would be an agent of salvation by making itself an offering for sin. As the days and months of his public ministry went by, Jesus saw more and more clearly that this image applied to him. Moreover, he realized that by accepting his passion and death as his destiny, he would reveal the love and power of God as he could in no other way.

Jesus' acceptance of his passion and death would show once and for all that no matter what horrible things evil human beings could do—and there is nothing worse than hanging an innocent man on a cross—the power of divine love is still greater. If God, the Father, could forgive that sin at the request of his Son, then all other sins can be forgiven.

THE PROBLEM OF SUFFERING AND DEATH

Here we confront the most troublesome and difficult question for those of us who believe in the kingdom of God. Why is there so much suffering, pain, heartbreak in the world—especially for the innocent? Sometimes we want to wag our fingers at God and shout, "Why did you make the world a place of such grief and torment?"

I don't know the answer to that question. I have asked it many times myself. This is what I do know, however: we won't find a satisfactory answer by imagining God as the one who lives far above our world of misery and doubt. If we believe in such a God, then the question is a very good one and there is no satisfactory answer to the problem of suffering and death.

The God revealed by Jesus, however, is one who does suffer and die. In the suffering, failure, heartbreak and dying of Jesus, God identifies with every single person in history who has suffered or died—whether innocently or justifiably. Our God, says Jesus from the cross, knows intimately about pain, disgrace, rejection, sorrow. No one can call out to this God: "You don't understand" or "You haven't suffered as I have" or "Why did you let them do this to me?" The answer comes back to us: "Look at Jesus, my beloved. Through him I have experienced failure, pain and death."

The message of God is the message of Jesus: "I say to you that listen, Love your enemies, do good to those who hate you, bless those who curse you, pray for those who abuse you. If anyone strikes you on the cheek, offer the other also; and from anyone who takes away your coat do not withhold even your shirt. Give to everyone who begs from you; and if anyone takes away your goods, do not ask for them again. Do to others as you would have them do to you" (Luke 6:27-31).

This teaching makes no sense in worldly terms. Following it leads to the cross. Yet somehow that path leads to the happiness of the kingdom of God. Paul says, "The message about the cross is foolishness to those who are perishing, but to us who are being saved it is the power of God" (1 Corinthians

1:18). For Paul, the cross reveals the true meaning of pain and the glory of God.

Jesus died an ignominious death on the cross. Does that mean God's role in human history ends in defeat? It might have, if it were not for the resurrection of Jesus—a light of hope, justice, peace, mercy, compassion and equality for the human race that shines in each of us who follow him.

Questions for Reflection or Discussion

1. Were you ever rejected by some individual or group? How did you handle it? What can you learn from the example of Jesus?

2. Which of the many reasons offered for the condemnation of Jesus by the authorities rings most true to you as the real one? Why?

3. Describe one time when you or someone you love accepted suffering or pain. What good things came out of it?

CHAPTER SEVEN

Jesus Is Risen

Do you really believe there is life after death? What do you think it is like? Jesus said, "I am the resurrection and the life" (John 11:25). What do you think he meant by that? This chapter explores the resurrection of Jesus and invites the reader to think about what happened and what it means to us now in our daily lives.

All religions are founded on two indisputable facts of human existence. First, we human beings are aware of our mortality. Neither the flowers in the field nor the stars in the sky nor the fish in the lake nor the animals in the forest realize they are all going to die someday. We humans know this from a very early age.

Second, among all cultures and at all times there arises a hope among people that death will not be the end of life but rather the beginning of something new. This remains a hope only–nothing of which we can be absolutely certain.

If you do not believe in life after death or if the question does not interest you, then you most likely do not need religion. In fact, you will probably reject the religious beliefs of your fellow human beings as cowardly and illusory.

The belief in life after death is always a hope founded on story and experience. That is true of all religions. Our Christian faith is founded on the story and experience of the rising of Jesus from the dead. It is the center of our belief in the kingdom of God.

WAS THE RESURRECTION REAL?

The first surviving written account of the resurrection comes almost thirty years after the event, from a man who wasn't even there! Paul writes the following in his first letter to the community at Corinth, which was in Greece, far from Jerusalem: "I handed on to you as of first importance what I in turn had received: that Christ died for our sins in accordance with the scriptures, and that he was buried, and that he was raised on the third day in accordance with the scriptures, and that he appeared to Cephas, then to the twelve. Then he appeared to more that five hundred brothers at one time, most of whom are still alive, though some have died. Then he appeared to James, then to all the apostles. Last of all, as to one untimely born, he appeared also to me" (1 Corinthians 15:3-8).

What do we mean by the resurrection of Jesus? First of all, we clearly do not mean that Jesus returned to life in the same condition as he was before his crucifixion. That would be resuscitation, which means to bring a person back to life minutes or possibly hours after the heart has stopped beating or the brain has shown no more activity. If Jesus had been resuscitated, then everyone who had known him before would have recognized him immediately after he rose. They would have said, "I'd have known him anywhere." But they didn't!

Mary Magdalene, for example, mistook him for a gardener. Others thought they had seen a ghost. Peter and John thought the man standing on the shore was a stranger. The disciples on the road to Emmaus recognized him only when he broke bread with them. Paul never saw Jesus at all.

Jesus had risen, yes. But he was somehow very different from before. For example, he appeared to different people at the same time. He entered rooms with locked doors. He appeared, according to St. Paul, in an imperishable, immortal body—one totally different from ours that die and decay. This is difficult for us to comprehend today. We want to ask, "Well, did he or didn't he really rise from the dead?" The answer to that question is unequivocally yes, but the question may be more complex than we are willing to admit.

What Really Happened, Then?

Let's tell the story again, but let us be careful. Because after Jesus dies, the story takes a dramatic turn. The death of Jesus on the cross is a historical fact. It was witnessed by many people, his enemies as well as his friends. If the facts of his death had been recorded as we do it today, we would know the exact time, place, day, month and year.

The rising of Jesus, however, is not history in that same way. It cannot be verified historically. Only those who loved Jesus and believed in him saw the risen Christ. No one else did. Does that mean it didn't really happen? No, it happened all right. But it was an event that occurred in a different dimension of human life—one not measured by time or the laws of nature.

An analogy from our experience may help us. A young girl whom you know and like tells you she has fallen in love. Do you ask her where it took place, at exactly what hour, and what caused it? Would you say, "Well, I didn't see it happen, so I don't believe you"? Of course you wouldn't! You know very well that falling in love cannot be measured or timed or proven the same way other ordinary events are. You would, however, look for the effects of love, which are observable—a new light in her eyes, changes in behavior that make her kinder and more tender with others.

Allow me to share a personal experience in this same realm. I had known Fr. Joseph Fitzpatrick for many years. He was a Jesuit and the Dean of the Sociology Department at Fordham University in New York City. No one knew the people of Latin America and loved them more than Joe Fitzpatrick. He was the kindest, holiest man I knew.

Father Fitzpatrick came down to Panama to visit me when I was a missionary there. He was deeply moved by the people and by our efforts to bring them the good news. We asked him to preside at our Eucharist one day. We gathered in a small room around a plain wooden table, about thirty priests, sisters and lay people in all.

He gave a little talk on the Scripture we had just read, and during the consecration he repeated the words of Jesus: "This is my body" and "This is the cup of my blood." At the moment of consecration, something happened to him. I couldn't believe my eyes, and I still can't describe it fully. All I can say is that his whole face lit up with a light that seemed to come from within. There's no doubt in my mind that he was transfigured before our very eyes.

After Mass was over, I went to each person present and asked, "Did you see something out of the ordinary?" Every person said that they had witnessed something very unusual. Each described the same occurrence differently, and some were far more touched than others, but the event did happen. On the other hand, if a policeman or some other person had been standing outside the door and watching us, I am certain he wouldn't have seen anything unusual at all—just a group of people standing around praying.

This little story was an experience that profoundly touched me and gave me an insight into what we mean by the resurrection. It was the power of God transforming the lifeless body of Jesus into the risen Christ—the same Jesus of Nazareth the disciples had always known, but now transformed into someone far greater and more glorious.

BLESSED ARE WE WHO HAVEN'T SEEN

Was Jesus raised from the dead? Somehow his disciples came to believe so, and they believed it in a real, concrete way.

The list of those who experienced the risen Christ is a long one. First was MaryMagdalene, then Peter and many of the others. Thomas was not among the disciples when Jesus first appeared to them, however, and he reacted much like we might have: "Unless I see the mark of the nails in his hands, and put my finger in the mark of the nails and put my hand in his side, I will not believe" (John 20:25).

But a week later Jesus appeared to the group again, and this time Thomas was with them.

It is interesting that Thomas did not carry through on his threat. Seeing Jesus alive, he could only say, "My Lord and my God!" (John 20:28).

Then Jesus sent a message hurtling down the centuries that I believe was intended directly for us: "Blessed are those who have not seen and yet have come to believe" (John 20:29). Why would those of us who "have not seen" be blessed (or happy)? I think it is because we don't have to worry about whether or not our eyes are playing tricks on us or we are dreaming—as the disciples surely must have.

We are more like Paul. He never knew Jesus in the mortal flesh and even persecuted those who followed the crucified Nazarene. But the spirit of Jesus he found in those disciples must have impressed him beyond measure, for it changed his life. He eventually came to see that it was the followers of Jesus who form his risen body: "You are the body of Christ and individually members of it" (1 Corinthians 12:27).

WHAT IS THE MEANING OF THE RESURRECTION?

What actually happened in the resurrection is less important than what it meant to Jesus' disciples and to us. What it means is that Jesus has overcome death, that his vision of the kingdom of God has been vindicated, and that it is now our job to carry it out.

Even as Jesus was about to ascend into heaven, some of the disciples were still unsure of what they were experiencing: "When they saw him, they worshipped him; but some doubted" (Matthew 28:17). This is comforting to me, since if they could doubt even as they looked upon the risen Jesus, it can't be all that wrong for us to wonder how it could happen or what really occurred.

Jesus told the disciples at that time: "All authority in heaven and earth has been given to me. Go therefore and make disciples of all nations, baptizing them in the name of the Father and of the Son and of the Holy Spirit, and teaching them to obey everything that I have commanded you. And remember, I am with you always, to the end of the age" (Matthew 28:18-20).

This then is the charge given by Jesus to his original followers: preach the kingdom, be my body and make it grow. These are the marching orders of Jesus that have inspired countless Christians to carry the message of Jesus to the ends of the earth.

Questions for Reflection or Discussion

1. What are the really important things that the resurrection of Jesus means in your life?

2. What do you think Jesus meant when he said, "Blessed are those who have not seen yet have come to believe"?

3. How do you carry out your job to spread Jesus' message about the kingdom of God?

CHAPTER EIGHT

Jesus in Christianity

Where do you encounter Jesus in your life—in prayer, in church, in work, in family, in giving to others? He said, "I am with you always, to the end of the age"(Matthew 28:20), but what does that mean? The early Christians had the same questions that we have, and they had to come to an understanding of how they were going to keep alive Jesus' vision of the kingdom of God. This chapter takes the reader through the first years of the Christian movement and suggests how we can continue to live out the message of Jesus today.

The risen Jesus gathered his followers around himself and commanded them to go out to all the world and preach the good news that the kingdom of God is coming and, in fact, has already begun in us. Tell the people, Jesus ordered, not to give up hope. God is already present among us, forgiving our sins and promising a new age of love and justice and peace.

Despite the considerable evidence to the contrary, the kingdom of God will be established. The way things are now is not God's last word on the way things will be. "For God all things are possible" (Mark 10:27), Jesus promised.

Inspired by that promise, the disciples of Jesus began to move out into the world. First they went to Judea, then to Galilee, to Samaria, to Asia Minor, and on and on. The first name given to these first followers was "the Way," the Way of Jesus, that is. Soon they began to be known as "Christians," after the Greek word for "messiah" or "the anointed one." Lastly they were called "the church," from a Greek word meaning "the gathered ones"—in this case those gathered around the person and message of Jesus Christ.

The word "church" now has several meanings. It can mean a building dedicated to Christian worship. It can also describe the governing structure of Christianity, both locally and universally. But first and foremost, Christianity is a movement of Jesus-people—those who believe that he is the Son of God, "the way, the truth and the life" (John 14:6)—walking with him and for him down the corridors of time. It is a movement that has spread and continues spreading to the four corners of the world (and to other worlds if and when that becomes possible). The Second Vatican Council described the church simply as "the Pilgrim People of God."

THE CHRISTIAN MOVEMENT

How has the Christian movement fared? Initially, it had phenomenal growth. On the day Jesus died, he had no more than a handful of followers—almost all of whom had run away. Within a few days, a core group of them had reassembled and began to grow—again by objective estimates—at the rate of forty percent every ten years. Within three hundred years, by some counts there were some six and a half million Christians—over half of the inhabitants of the Roman Empire!

How did this growth happen, and why? For one thing, the disciples of Jesus were able to use the network of Jewish communities that were present in almost every town and city of the Roman Empire to spread the word. Some say that Jews represented ten percent of the Roman citizens at the time. As was their custom, the Jewish people in each town opened their homes and synagogues to fellow Jewish visitors from all over the world. Thus the Jesus followers were welcomed and given an opportunity to tell the Jesus story. It was a simple method of networking and a very successful one.

A second reason for the remarkable success of the early Christian movement was that the Christians were absolutely convinced of the resurrection—not only that of Jesus but of their own as well. They had no fear of death. That made them carefree risk-takers, people who laughed at death and made great sacrifices with a smile. They were something new and very attractive in the ancient world.

A third reason for the rapid growth of Christianity was the extraordinary respect and equality Christians accorded to those whom the society of the day oppressed or put down. For example, the centerpiece of early Christian worship was the communal meal. They gathered every Saturday night for a fraternal supper—not merely a symbolic one of bread and wine that we have now, but a full meal. The poor brought the little they had. The more affluent brought a good amount of food. The poor came away thankful because this probably was the only substantial meal of the week. The rich were grateful also, because they had an opportunity to share their abundance in a meaningful way. Women, servants and slaves were deeply impressed because they were treated as equals in the family of God.

Fourth, Christians quickly became primary caregivers in a society almost overwhelmed by sickness and disease. The towns and cities of the ancient world were pest holes. The water supply was often contaminated. There were no sewers or drainage systems. The poor people lived in over-crowded rickety tenements. There were no clinics or hospitals. It was common for families to leave desperately sick people out on the street to die. Christians never did that. They took care of the sick—their own and strangers. The situation got much worse in times of epidemics and plague, which were regular occurrences then. This extraordinary care of the sick gave rise to the famous saying, "See how these Christians love one another."

Finally, the Christians inherited from their Jewish heritage a high standard of morality. The chosen people of God had been commanded not to steal, nor lie, nor commit adultery.

They were told not to tolerate injustice, such as the abuse of women, children and slaves. It was a very lofty ethic that was at once personal, familial and communal. Christians took on this demanding value system freely, not because they were forced to do so but because it was God's way. Furthermore, they reasoned that they could hardly expect the pagan world to accept the message of Jesus unless they themselves lived as Jesus had commanded them—as a holy, just and faithful people.

EARLY CHRISTIAN LIFE

The early Christians believed in the kingdom of God—the imminent coming of peace, justice and fairness. Did they think they were the kingdom itself? No, they knew the reign of God was wider, deeper and holier than they. They knew they weren't perfect. They sometimes did not live up to their high ideals. But when they did sin, they forgave one another and started over again, not holding others in their weaknesses and failings as so many of their neighbors did.

They did believe that they, as a church, were the great sign of the kingdom of God, a sacred sign of universal salvation for all the world. They believed that they were the new Israel, the keepers of the promises made to the ancient Hebrews, the witnesses of the "new covenant" with God.

When others accepted Jesus and all he taught, the Christians welcomed them by means of baptism. You remember that John the Baptist baptized people in the Jordan River. He would first have them admit to their sins—their own personal sins but also, more importantly, the sins of their nation. Then he would have them wade through the river from one side to the other, clearly evoking the memory of the people of God going through the water of the Red Sea and coming out a new people, the people of God.

Christians believed that every human being is born in the image and likeness of God and is therefore a son or daughter of God. By baptism, however, we are born again into the life of Christ and become members of the church, the new chosen people—chosen to proclaim the good news, privileged to live and die as a sign of the kingdom of God in our world.

The early Christian community prayed hard and often. Their prayer, however, was very different from that of their contemporaries. They offered no animal sacrifices. Instead the central act of worship was the communal supper. In that special meal, always one of thanksgiving (that's what the word "Eucharist" means), the believers did three things.

First, they remembered the past, all the great things God had done in human history, especially in the person of Jesus. Second, they celebrated the presence of Christ among them and their loving communion with him and with one another. Finally, they renewed their faith in God and their hope in the coming of the reign of God to all peoples. It was from this prayerful meal that they derived the courage to proclaim their faith to a world that was hostile, the strength to take care of one another and to forgive one another, and the will to resist the powers of their day—the forces of evil, violence, abuse, hatred.

Just as the ancient Hebrews had stood up to Egypt, so the early Christians stood up to Rome. For example, they refused to offer incense to idols.

They also adamantly refused to serve in the army, because they considered the army to be an evil system. Soldiers of the time received little or no pay. Rather, in return for their service they were allowed to loot and pillage the people they conquered. A commander such as Julius Caesar, for example, got very rich by selling off conquered peoples as slaves. Christians refused to participate in an enterprise so cruel and immoral.

The struggle between the early church and the Roman authorities was seemingly an uneven fight. The blood of martyrs was spilled everywhere. But in the end, the faith of the early Christians won out and changed their world.

Every succeeding age—including our own—has presented a different challenge to the movement of Christianity. At times the movement has faltered and failed. Christianity, in its frequent failures to live in the spirit of Jesus, has all too often caused scandal, suffering and disappointment to all of us.

At other times, the witness of Christians has made the world a better place for all. No other movement in history has done more to lift humanity to heights of holiness and justice, nor done more to advance learning and the arts.

We today will just have to live with this tension between the good and the bad, the successes and the failures of Christianity, confident that God has "set forth in Christ, as a plan for the fullness of time, to gather up all things in him, things in heaven and things on earth" (Ephesians 1:10).

Questions for Reflection or Discussion

1. What about early Christianity is most appealing to you? Why? How could you incorporate more of those qualities into your own Christian life?

2. Which images of the church are most helpful to you? Can you think of any other images that might be used? Name them.

3. What are the major obstacles and challenges facing Christianity today? What are you doing or could you be doing to help overcome or meet them?

Conclusion

This little book on Jesus and his message has only scratched the surface. Part of being a follower of Jesus is to learn as much as we can about who he is and what he stands for. This can be done by reading and studying the Bible, by reading the many good books that are available on Jesus and his teaching, by participating in ongoing adult religious education, and by building community with others who are trying to follow him in their daily lives.

Whereas Jesus and his first companions were a tiny fraction of the world's population, we Christians today are more than a billion strong and can be a major force in human history. All over the world, we see the cross high above churches, schools, orphanages, hospitals, nursing homes and food pantries, as well as on the walls of millions of homes. Once again, in our own time and place, we must look at ourselves and ask whether we understand and live the mysteries revealed in the life and death of Jesus Christ.

Do we believe in the kingdom of God on earth and its ultimate victory? Do we do our best to proclaim it by our lives as well as by our words?

Do we believe in the church as the great sacred sign of universal salvation?

Do we present in our faith community the lifestyle of Jesus—his love, compassion, fairness, equality, forgiveness?

Do we hate violence of every kind and work and pray for peace?

Do we strive for unity among all Christians and all people of good faith and good will? Are we willing to make sacrifices, to endure pain, suffering and heartbreak, to make up "what is lacking in Christ's afflictions" (Colossians 1:24), as Paul put it? Do we really believe in the cross of Jesus—that by suffering and dying with Jesus we shall overcome the evil of the world?

Can we stand with Jesus and look at our world as he looked with love and sorrow on Jerusalem? There is much good in our world, but there is also much evil, so prevalent that it not only traps us into conforming but it also blinds us to the truth. We don't even realize that in many ways we are caught up in a world that is, in large part, anti-Christian.

We live in a world that values people for what they possess. Is that the way of Christ?

We live in a world so competitive that the most successful and the most aggressive get the rewards of fame, attention, wealth. How about the losers—left on the side of the road despised, abandoned, pitied? Do we respect and care for the "little ones" as Jesus called them—the poor, the sick, the homeless, the immigrants, the minorities, all those different from ourselves?

We live in a world that makes money out of everything—sex, violence and even religion. Are we too money mad and pleasure crazy?

Our world wastes and violates the abundant resources of the earth. Are we sorry for our sins against nature? Do we fight to protect its life and beauty?

Christianity, remember, is a movement based on a single person and his message. It is because of Jesus that we know who we are--forgiven sons and daughters of God. It is because of Jesus that we have an unconquerable faith in the future.

Here is my image of where we are all headed. One day we shall be seated—all of us—at a great table with Jesus. All the great saints of history will be there, as well as all the "little ones" the Lord loved so much. At that moment, Jesus will be about to celebrate his final victory and offer to his Father a people inclusive of all and united in love. Then, I see the door opening. Who is the very last person to come to the banquet?

It is Judas. Jesus embraces him. At last, we are all together.

This is the kingdom of God—the way God wants things to be, history as God wants it to turn out, God's vision for the world. Do we want to make it our vision as well? We can if we share—right now, today, in our daily lives—the exciting challenge of Jesus' message and the holiness of his death and resurrection.

ALSO AVAILABLE

Life in Christ
Revs. Gerard Weber and James Killgallon

Using the traditional question-and-answer format, *Life in Christ* offers a scripturally-based presentation of the teachings and practices of the Catholic Church. (316-page paperback, $5.95)

Becoming Catholic: Even If You Happen to Be One
Revs. Gerard Weber and James Killgallon

An experientially-based overview of basic beliefs for active Catholics, those considering joining the Catholic Church, and inactive Catholics willing to take another, more adult look at their faith. (216-page paperback, $6.95)

The Catholic Sourcebook, Revised Edition
Rev. Peter Klein

Filled with clear, concise, accurate information on scripture, sacraments, doctrine, the liturgical year, devotions, saints and heroes, councils and popes, church history, religious practices and customs, Catholic symbols, and much more. (512-page paperback, $18.95)

Catholics and Fundamentalists
Rev. Martin Pable, OFM Cap.

The straightforward and practical answers that Catholics need to understand Fundamentalism, along with wise guidance and practical suggestions for reaching out to Fundamentalists in a spirit of Christian charity. (96-page paperback, $5.95)

**Available from Christian Booksellers
or call 800-397-2282**